D1294130

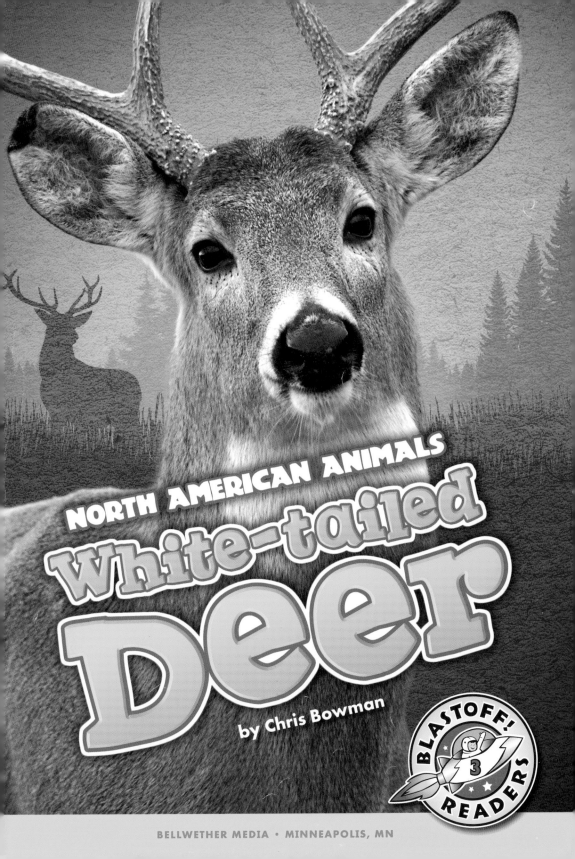

NORTH AMERICAN ANIMALS

White-tailed Deer

by Chris Bowman

BLASTOFF!
3
READERS

BELLWETHER MEDIA • MINNEAPOLIS, MN

Note to Librarians, Teachers, and Parents:

Blastoff! Readers are carefully developed by literacy experts and combine standards-based content with developmentally appropriate text.

Level 1 provides the most support through repetition of high-frequency words, light text, predictable sentence patterns, and strong visual support.

Level 2 offers early readers a bit more challenge through varied simple sentences, increased text load, and less repetition of high-frequency words.

Level 3 advances early-fluent readers toward fluency through increased text and concept load, less reliance on visuals, longer sentences, and more literary language.

Level 4 builds reading stamina by providing more text per page, increased use of punctuation, greater variation in sentence patterns, and increasingly challenging vocabulary.

Level 5 encourages children to move from "learning to read" to "reading to learn" by providing even more text, varied writing styles, and less familiar topics.

Whichever book is right for your reader, Blastoff! Readers are the perfect books to build confidence and encourage a love of reading that will last a lifetime!

This edition first published in 2015 by Bellwether Media, Inc.

No part of this publication may be reproduced in whole or in part without written permission of the publisher. For information regarding permission, write to Bellwether Media, Inc., Attention: Permissions Department, 5357 Penn Avenue South, Minneapolis, MN 55419.

Library of Congress Cataloging-in-Publication Data

Bowman, Chris, 1990- author.
  White-tailed Deer / by Chris Bowman.
     pages cm. – (Blastoff! Readers. North American Animals)
  Includes bibliographical references and index.
  Summary: "Simple text and full-color photography introduce beginning readers to white-tailed deer. Developed by literacy experts for students in kindergarten through third grade"– Provided by publisher.
  Audience: Ages 5-8.
  Audience: K to Grade 3.
  ISBN 978-1-62617-195-4 (hardcover : alk. paper)
  1. White-tailed deer–Juvenile literature. [1. Deer.] I. Title.
  QL737.U55B6385 2015
  599.65'2–dc23
                                                          2014041352

Printed in the United States of America, North Mankato, MN.

Table of Contents

What Are White-tailed Deer?

White-tailed deer are hoofed **mammals**. They live throughout much of Canada, the United States, and Mexico.

In the Wild

N
W E
S

Extinct

Extinct in the Wild

Critically Endangered

Endangered

Vulnerable

Near Threatened

Least Concern

white-tailed deer range =

conservation status: least concern

These deer often hide in forests. They are also found in deserts, prairies, and swamps.

Identify a White-tailed Deer

white tail white on behind white on face

White-tailed deer have reddish brown coats in the summer. Their fur fades to grayish brown in the winter.

6

They have white patches by their eyes, nose, and throat. Their bellies are also white.

These deer are named for the white fur on the underside of their tails.

They raise their tails to show the white when scared. This warns other deer that danger may be near.

Finding Food

White-tailed deer search for food in the evening and early morning. They are **herbivores**.

On the Menu

corn

pine needles

maple leaves

acorns

apples

mushrooms

In the summer, they eat leaves, fruits, and mushrooms. They chew on nuts and corn in the fall. Twigs and bark are winter foods.

Animals to Avoid

gray wolves

coyotes

mountain lions

black bears

White-tailed deer must be ready to run from **predators**. Even in thick forests, they can run up to 30 miles (48 kilometers) per hour! This is usually fast enough to outrun bears, wolves, and other animals.

Male white-tailed deer are called **bucks**. They grow to be bigger than females, or **does**.

Size of a White-tailed Deer

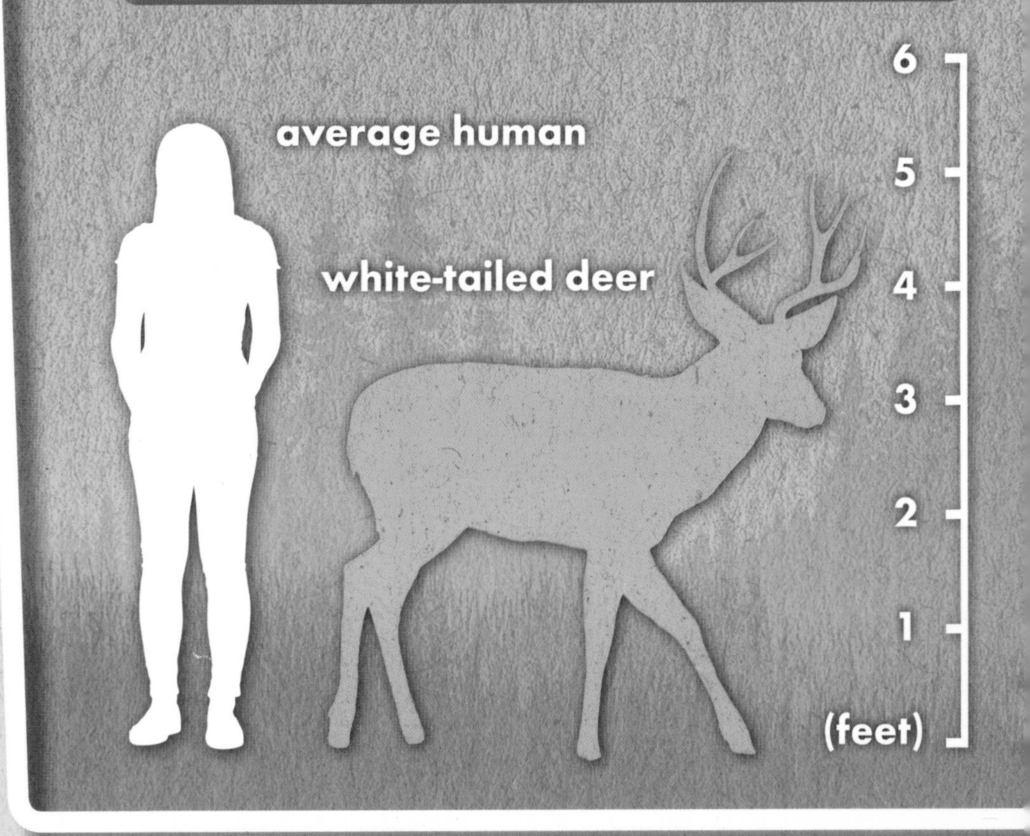

average human

white-tailed deer

6
5
4
3
2
1
(feet)

Bucks grow up to 6 feet (1.8 meters) long. Their shoulders are about 3 feet (0.9 meters) from the ground. They weigh up to 300 pounds (136 kilograms).

15

Every spring, bucks grow a new set of **antlers**.

They use them to fight over does. Then the antlers fall off in winter.

Mom and Fawns

A doe gives birth to up to three **fawns** at a time. White spots cover the fawns' backs. These **camouflage** them from predators.

Baby Facts

Name for babies:	fawns
Size of litter:	1 to 3 fawns
Length of pregnancy:	6 to 7 months
Time spent with parents:	1 to 2 years

At 3 to 4 months old, fawns usually lose their spots.

They stay with mom for up to two years. Then they have fawns of their own!

Glossary

antlers—the branched horns on male deer

bucks—male deer

camouflage—to hide an animal by helping it blend in with the surroundings

does—female deer

fawns—baby deer

herbivores—animals that only eat plants

mammals—warm-blooded animals that have backbones and feed their young milk

predators—animals that hunt other animals for food

To Learn More

AT THE LIBRARY

Callery, Sean. *Forest*. New York, N.Y.: Kingfisher, 2012.

Magby, Meryl. *White-tailed Deer*. New York, N.Y.: PowerKids Press, 2014.

O'Brien, Bridget. *Deer Eat and Grow*. Minneapolis, Minn.: Magic Wagon, 2015.

ON THE WEB
Learning more about white-tailed deer is as easy as 1, 2, 3.

1. Go to www.factsurfer.com.

2. Enter "white-tailed deer" into the search box.

3. Click the "Surf" button and you will see a list of related web sites.

With factsurfer.com, finding more information is just a click away.

Index

The images in this book are reproduced through the courtesy of: Tom Reichner, front cover, p. 6 (top right);
Charles Brutlag, pp. 4-5; James Marvin Phelps, p. 6 (top left); Minden Pictures/ SuperStock, p. 6 (top center);
JAMES PIERCE, p. 6 (bottom); Mike Rogal, p. 7; Mike McVittie, p. 8; Minden Pictures/ Corbis, pp. 9, 19;
Gary Griffen/ Age Fotostock, pp. 10-11; oksana2010, p. 11 (top left); Kesu, p. 11 (top right); Lightstpring, p. 11
(center left); Hurst Photo, p. 11 (center right); baibaz, p. 11 (bottom left); Sergey Rusakov, p. 11 (bottom right);
Maxim Kulko, p. 12 (top left); Cynthia Kidwell, p. 12 (top right); Ultrashock, p. 12 (bottom left); vblinov,
p. 12 (bottom right); Tom Uhlman/ Alamy, pp. 12-13; Michael Francis Photography/ Animals Animals, p. 14;
Lightwriter1949, p. 16; Mike Rogal, pp. 16-17; W. Perry Conway/ Animals Animals, pp. 20-21.